50 World's Best Meatballs Recipes

By: Kelly Johnson

Table of Contents

- Classic Italian Meatballs
- Swedish Meatballs with Gravy
- Spicy Lamb Meatballs with Mint Yogurt
- Turkey Meatballs in Marinara Sauce
- BBQ Beef Meatballs
- Greek Meatballs with Tzatziki
- Teriyaki Chicken Meatballs
- Baked Meatballs with Mozzarella
- Meatball Sub Sandwiches
- Asian Pork Meatballs with Ginger
- Beef and Spinach Meatballs
- Meatballs in Creamy Mushroom Sauce
- Moroccan Meatballs with Couscous
- BBQ Pork Meatballs
- Venison Meatballs with Garlic and Rosemary
- Meatballs in Sweet and Sour Sauce
- Spicy Buffalo Chicken Meatballs
- Chicken Parmesan Meatballs
- Slow Cooker Meatballs in Tomato Sauce
- Eggplant and Beef Meatballs
- Meatball and Potato Stew
- Korean BBQ Meatballs
- Parmesan and Ricotta Meatballs
- Beef and Bacon Meatballs
- Sweet and Spicy Teriyaki Meatballs
- Lamb Meatballs with Feta and Olives
- Italian Sausage and Beef Meatballs
- Thai Chicken Meatballs with Peanut Sauce
- Meatball Soup with Veggies
- Almond-Crusted Meatballs
- Asian-style Turkey Meatballs
- Italian Meatballs with Peppers and Onions
- Spicy Chorizo Meatballs
- Swedish Meatballs with Lingonberry Sauce
- Beef and Pork Meatballs with Garlic Butter

- BBQ Chicken Meatballs
- Spaghetti and Meatballs
- Zesty Cilantro Lime Meatballs
- Coconut Curry Meatballs
- Cajun Shrimp Meatballs
- Meatball and Polenta Bake
- Classic Beef Meatballs in Gravy
- Moroccan-spiced Beef Meatballs
- Italian Meatballs in a Red Wine Sauce
- Sweet Chili Chicken Meatballs
- Pork and Apple Meatballs
- Cilantro and Lime Pork Meatballs
- Meatball Bolognese
- Mediterranean Lamb Meatballs
- Grilled Beef Meatballs with Chimichurri

Classic Italian Meatballs

Ingredients:

- 1 lb ground beef
- 1/2 cup breadcrumbs
- 1/4 cup grated Parmesan cheese
- 1 large egg
- 2 cloves garlic, minced
- 1/4 cup fresh parsley, chopped
- 1 tsp dried oregano
- Salt and pepper to taste
- 1 1/2 cups marinara sauce

Instructions:

1. **Mix Ingredients**: In a large bowl, combine the ground beef, breadcrumbs, Parmesan, egg, garlic, parsley, oregano, salt, and pepper. Mix until fully combined.
2. **Form Meatballs**: Shape the mixture into 1-inch meatballs and place them on a baking sheet.
3. **Cook Meatballs**: Bake in a preheated 375°F (190°C) oven for 15-20 minutes until browned and cooked through.
4. **Simmer in Sauce**: Heat marinara sauce in a pan and add the meatballs, cooking for an additional 5-10 minutes. Serve with pasta or on their own.

Swedish Meatballs with Gravy

Ingredients:

- 1 lb ground beef
- 1/2 lb ground pork
- 1/2 cup breadcrumbs
- 1/4 cup milk
- 1 egg
- 1/4 cup finely chopped onion
- Salt and pepper to taste
- 2 tbsp butter
- 2 tbsp flour
- 2 cups beef broth
- 1/2 cup heavy cream

Instructions:

1. **Mix Meatball Ingredients**: In a large bowl, combine ground beef, ground pork, breadcrumbs, milk, egg, onion, salt, and pepper. Shape into meatballs.
2. **Cook Meatballs**: In a large skillet, heat butter over medium heat. Cook meatballs until browned on all sides, then remove from skillet.
3. **Make Gravy**: In the same skillet, add flour and cook for 1 minute. Gradually whisk in beef broth and bring to a simmer. Stir in cream and cook until the gravy thickens.
4. **Simmer Meatballs in Gravy**: Return meatballs to the skillet and simmer in the gravy for 10 minutes. Serve with mashed potatoes.

Spicy Lamb Meatballs with Mint Yogurt

Ingredients:

- 1 lb ground lamb
- 1/2 cup breadcrumbs
- 1/4 cup chopped fresh mint
- 1 tsp ground cumin
- 1 tsp ground coriander
- 1/2 tsp cayenne pepper
- 1 egg
- Salt and pepper to taste
- 1/2 cup plain Greek yogurt
- 1 tbsp fresh mint, chopped
- 1 tsp lemon juice

Instructions:

1. **Mix Meatball Ingredients**: In a bowl, combine lamb, breadcrumbs, chopped mint, cumin, coriander, cayenne pepper, egg, salt, and pepper. Shape into meatballs.
2. **Cook Meatballs**: Heat a skillet with a little oil over medium heat. Cook meatballs until browned and cooked through, about 8-10 minutes.
3. **Make Mint Yogurt Sauce**: In a small bowl, combine Greek yogurt, fresh mint, and lemon juice.
4. **Serve**: Serve meatballs with the mint yogurt sauce on the side.

Turkey Meatballs in Marinara Sauce

Ingredients:

- 1 lb ground turkey
- 1/2 cup breadcrumbs
- 1/4 cup grated Parmesan cheese
- 1 egg
- 2 cloves garlic, minced
- 1 tsp dried basil
- Salt and pepper to taste
- 2 cups marinara sauce

Instructions:

1. **Mix Meatball Ingredients**: In a bowl, combine ground turkey, breadcrumbs, Parmesan, egg, garlic, basil, salt, and pepper. Shape into meatballs.
2. **Cook Meatballs**: Bake meatballs in a preheated 375°F (190°C) oven for 15-20 minutes until browned.
3. **Simmer in Sauce**: Heat marinara sauce in a large pan. Add meatballs to the sauce and simmer for 10-15 minutes. Serve over pasta or on their own.

BBQ Beef Meatballs

Ingredients:

- 1 lb ground beef
- 1/4 cup breadcrumbs
- 1/4 cup BBQ sauce
- 1 egg
- 1/4 cup chopped green onions
- Salt and pepper to taste
- 1/2 cup BBQ sauce for glazing

Instructions:

1. **Mix Meatball Ingredients**: In a bowl, combine ground beef, breadcrumbs, BBQ sauce, egg, green onions, salt, and pepper. Shape into meatballs.
2. **Cook Meatballs**: Bake in a preheated 375°F (190°C) oven for 15-20 minutes until browned.
3. **Glaze with BBQ Sauce**: Brush BBQ sauce over the cooked meatballs and return to the oven for 5-10 minutes. Serve with extra BBQ sauce.

Greek Meatballs with Tzatziki

Ingredients:

- 1 lb ground lamb or beef
- 1/2 cup breadcrumbs
- 1/4 cup chopped fresh parsley
- 1 egg
- 2 cloves garlic, minced
- 1 tsp dried oregano
- Salt and pepper to taste
- 1/2 cup Greek yogurt
- 1 tbsp cucumber, grated
- 1 tsp lemon juice
- 1 tbsp olive oil

Instructions:

1. **Mix Meatball Ingredients**: In a bowl, combine ground lamb, breadcrumbs, parsley, egg, garlic, oregano, salt, and pepper. Shape into meatballs.
2. **Cook Meatballs**: Heat olive oil in a skillet over medium heat. Cook meatballs until browned on all sides and cooked through, about 8-10 minutes.
3. **Make Tzatziki**: In a small bowl, combine Greek yogurt, grated cucumber, lemon juice, salt, and pepper.
4. **Serve**: Serve meatballs with tzatziki on the side.

Teriyaki Chicken Meatballs

Ingredients:

- 1 lb ground chicken
- 1/4 cup breadcrumbs
- 2 tbsp soy sauce
- 1 tbsp honey
- 1/2 tsp ginger, grated
- 1 clove garlic, minced
- 1 egg
- 2 tbsp chopped green onions
- 1/4 cup teriyaki sauce for glazing

Instructions:

1. **Mix Meatball Ingredients**: In a bowl, combine ground chicken, breadcrumbs, soy sauce, honey, ginger, garlic, egg, and green onions. Shape into meatballs.
2. **Cook Meatballs**: Bake meatballs in a preheated 375°F (190°C) oven for 15-20 minutes.
3. **Glaze with Teriyaki Sauce**: Brush teriyaki sauce over the cooked meatballs and return to the oven for 5-10 minutes. Serve with rice or vegetables.

Baked Meatballs with Mozzarella

Ingredients:

- 1 lb ground beef or pork
- 1/4 cup breadcrumbs
- 1/4 cup grated Parmesan cheese
- 1 egg
- 1 tsp Italian seasoning
- 2 cups marinara sauce
- 8 oz mozzarella cheese, shredded

Instructions:

1. **Mix Meatball Ingredients**: In a bowl, combine ground meat, breadcrumbs, Parmesan, egg, and Italian seasoning. Shape into meatballs.
2. **Bake Meatballs**: Place meatballs on a baking sheet and bake at 375°F (190°C) for 15-20 minutes.
3. **Top with Marinara and Mozzarella**: Pour marinara sauce over the meatballs and sprinkle with mozzarella cheese. Return to the oven for 5-10 minutes until the cheese is melted. Serve with pasta or on its own.

Meatball Sub Sandwiches

Ingredients:

- 1 batch of Italian meatballs (from the previous recipe)
- 4 sub rolls
- 1 1/2 cups marinara sauce
- 1 cup shredded mozzarella cheese
- 1/4 cup grated Parmesan cheese
- Fresh basil (optional)

Instructions:

1. Prepare Meatballs: Cook Italian meatballs according to the previous recipe.
2. Assemble Subs: Slice sub rolls and warm them in the oven for a few minutes.
3. Build Sandwiches: Place meatballs on the rolls, cover with marinara sauce, and sprinkle with mozzarella and Parmesan cheese.
4. Melt Cheese: Broil in the oven for 2-3 minutes until the cheese is melted and bubbly. Garnish with fresh basil if desired. Serve immediately.

Asian Pork Meatballs with Ginger

Ingredients:

- 1 lb ground pork
- 1/4 cup breadcrumbs
- 2 tbsp soy sauce
- 1 tbsp hoisin sauce
- 1 tsp ground ginger
- 2 cloves garlic, minced
- 1 egg
- 1 tbsp sesame oil
- 1/4 cup green onions, chopped
- 1 tbsp sesame seeds

Instructions:

1. Mix Meatball Ingredients: In a bowl, combine ground pork, breadcrumbs, soy sauce, hoisin sauce, ginger, garlic, egg, and sesame oil. Shape into meatballs.
2. Cook Meatballs: Heat a skillet over medium heat and cook meatballs until browned on all sides and cooked through, about 8-10 minutes.
3. Serve: Garnish with chopped green onions and sesame seeds. Serve with steamed rice or in lettuce wraps.

Beef and Spinach Meatballs

Ingredients:

- 1 lb ground beef
- 1/2 cup fresh spinach, chopped
- 1/4 cup breadcrumbs
- 1/4 cup grated Parmesan cheese
- 1 egg
- 1 tsp garlic powder
- 1/2 tsp dried oregano
- Salt and pepper to taste
- Marinara sauce (optional)

Instructions:

1. Mix Meatball Ingredients: In a bowl, combine ground beef, spinach, breadcrumbs, Parmesan, egg, garlic powder, oregano, salt, and pepper. Shape into meatballs.
2. Cook Meatballs: Bake meatballs in a preheated 375°F (190°C) oven for 15-20 minutes until browned and cooked through.
3. Serve: Serve with marinara sauce on pasta or on their own.

Meatballs in Creamy Mushroom Sauce

Ingredients:

- 1 batch of Italian meatballs (from the previous recipe)
- 2 tbsp butter
- 1 cup mushrooms, sliced
- 2 cloves garlic, minced
- 1 cup heavy cream
- 1/2 cup beef broth
- 1 tbsp Dijon mustard
- Salt and pepper to taste
- Fresh parsley, chopped
  Instructions:

1. Cook Meatballs: Prepare meatballs according to your preferred recipe.
2. Make Mushroom Sauce: In a skillet, melt butter over medium heat. Add sliced mushrooms and garlic, and sauté until tender.
3. Simmer Sauce: Add beef broth and bring to a simmer. Stir in heavy cream and Dijon mustard, cooking until the sauce thickens, about 5 minutes.
4. Combine: Add meatballs to the sauce and simmer for an additional 10 minutes.
5. Serve: Garnish with fresh parsley and serve with mashed potatoes or rice.

Moroccan Meatballs with Couscous

Ingredients:

- 1 lb ground beef or lamb
- 1/4 cup breadcrumbs
- 1/4 cup raisins
- 1 tsp ground cumin
- 1 tsp ground cinnamon
- 1/2 tsp paprika
- 1 egg
- Salt and pepper to taste
- 1 1/2 cups couscous
- 1/2 cup chopped fresh cilantro
- 1 tbsp olive oil

Instructions:

1. Mix Meatball Ingredients: In a bowl, combine ground meat, breadcrumbs, raisins, cumin, cinnamon, paprika, egg, salt, and pepper. Shape into meatballs.
2. Cook Meatballs: In a skillet, heat olive oil over medium heat. Cook meatballs until browned on all sides and cooked through, about 8-10 minutes.
3. Prepare Couscous: Cook couscous according to package instructions. Fluff with a fork and stir in chopped cilantro.
4. Serve: Serve meatballs on a bed of couscous, garnished with additional cilantro.

BBQ Pork Meatballs

Ingredients:

- 1 lb ground pork
- 1/2 cup breadcrumbs
- 1/4 cup chopped green onions
- 1 egg
- 1/4 cup BBQ sauce
- 1/4 tsp garlic powder
- 1/4 tsp onion powder
- Salt and pepper to taste
- 1/2 cup BBQ sauce for glazing
   Instructions:

1. Mix Meatball Ingredients: In a bowl, combine ground pork, breadcrumbs, green onions, egg, BBQ sauce, garlic powder, onion powder, salt, and pepper. Shape into meatballs.
2. Cook Meatballs: Bake meatballs in a preheated 375°F (190°C) oven for 15-20 minutes.
3. Glaze with BBQ Sauce: Brush meatballs with BBQ sauce and return to the oven for an additional 5 minutes.
4. Serve: Serve with additional BBQ sauce for dipping.

Venison Meatballs with Garlic and Rosemary

Ingredients:

- 1 lb ground venison
- 1/4 cup breadcrumbs
- 2 cloves garlic, minced
- 1 tbsp fresh rosemary, chopped
- 1 egg
- Salt and pepper to taste
- 1 tbsp olive oil

Instructions:

1. Mix Meatball Ingredients: In a bowl, combine ground venison, breadcrumbs, garlic, rosemary, egg, salt, and pepper. Shape into meatballs.
2. Cook Meatballs: Heat olive oil in a skillet over medium heat. Cook meatballs until browned and cooked through, about 8-10 minutes.
3. Serve: Serve with roasted vegetables or over pasta.

Meatballs in Sweet and Sour Sauce

Ingredients:

- 1 batch of Italian meatballs (from the previous recipe)
- 1 cup pineapple chunks (with juice)
- 1/2 cup ketchup
- 1/4 cup soy sauce
- 1/4 cup rice vinegar
- 2 tbsp brown sugar
- 1 tsp garlic powder
- 1 tsp ginger, grated

Instructions:
1. Prepare Meatballs: Cook Italian meatballs as desired.
2. Make Sweet and Sour Sauce: In a small saucepan, combine pineapple chunks, ketchup, soy sauce, rice vinegar, brown sugar, garlic powder, and ginger. Bring to a simmer and cook for 5-7 minutes.
3. Combine: Add meatballs to the sweet and sour sauce and simmer for an additional 10 minutes.
4. Serve: Serve meatballs with rice or in a sandwich bun.

Spicy Buffalo Chicken Meatballs

Ingredients:

- 1 lb ground chicken
- 1/4 cup breadcrumbs
- 1/4 cup finely chopped celery
- 1 egg
- 1/2 cup buffalo sauce
- 1 tbsp garlic powder
- 1/2 tsp cayenne pepper
- Salt and pepper to taste
- 1/4 cup blue cheese crumbles (optional)

Instructions:

1. Mix Meatball Ingredients: In a bowl, combine ground chicken, breadcrumbs, celery, egg, buffalo sauce, garlic powder, cayenne pepper, salt, and pepper. Shape into meatballs.
2. Cook Meatballs: Bake meatballs in a preheated 375°F (190°C) oven for 15-20 minutes, until cooked through.
3. Serve: Toss meatballs in extra buffalo sauce and top with blue cheese crumbles if desired. Serve with celery and a side of ranch or blue cheese dressing.

Chicken Parmesan Meatballs

Ingredients:

- 1 lb ground chicken
- 1/2 cup breadcrumbs
- 1/4 cup grated Parmesan cheese
- 1/2 tsp dried oregano
- 1/2 tsp garlic powder
- 1 egg
- 1 1/2 cups marinara sauce
- 1 cup shredded mozzarella cheese

Instructions:

1. Mix Meatball Ingredients: In a bowl, combine ground chicken, breadcrumbs, Parmesan, oregano, garlic powder, and egg. Shape into meatballs.
2. Cook Meatballs: Bake meatballs in a preheated 375°F (190°C) oven for 15-20 minutes until golden and cooked through.
3. Assemble: Heat marinara sauce in a skillet, add meatballs, and simmer for 5-10 minutes.
4. Top with Cheese: Sprinkle mozzarella on top of meatballs, cover, and cook for 2-3 minutes until melted. Serve with pasta or on a sub roll.

Slow Cooker Meatballs in Tomato Sauce

Ingredients:

- 1 lb ground beef or pork
- 1/4 cup breadcrumbs
- 1/4 cup grated Parmesan cheese
- 1/2 tsp garlic powder
- 1 egg
- 2 cups marinara sauce
- 1 tsp dried basil
- 1/2 tsp red pepper flakes (optional)

Instructions:

1. Prepare Meatballs: In a bowl, combine ground meat, breadcrumbs, Parmesan, garlic powder, egg, salt, and pepper. Shape into meatballs.
2. Cook in Slow Cooker: Place meatballs in a slow cooker and cover with marinara sauce. Add basil and red pepper flakes if using.
3. Cook: Cover and cook on low for 4-6 hours or on high for 2-3 hours.
4. Serve: Serve meatballs with pasta or on sub rolls for meatball sandwiches.

Eggplant and Beef Meatballs

Ingredients:

- 1/2 lb ground beef
- 1/2 lb eggplant, peeled and finely chopped
- 1/4 cup breadcrumbs
- 1 egg
- 2 cloves garlic, minced
- 1/2 tsp dried oregano
- Salt and pepper to taste
  Instructions:

1. Prepare Eggplant: Heat a skillet over medium heat and sauté chopped eggplant until tender, about 5-7 minutes.
2. Mix Meatball Ingredients: In a bowl, combine ground beef, eggplant, breadcrumbs, egg, garlic, oregano, salt, and pepper. Shape into meatballs.
3. Cook Meatballs: Bake meatballs in a preheated 375°F (190°C) oven for 15-20 minutes or until browned and cooked through.
4. Serve: Serve with marinara sauce and pasta or over a bed of greens.

Meatball and Potato Stew

Ingredients:

- 1 lb meatballs (any style)
- 4 medium potatoes, peeled and diced
- 1 onion, chopped
- 2 cloves garlic, minced
- 4 cups beef broth
- 2 carrots, sliced
- 1 tsp dried thyme
- Salt and pepper to taste
- Fresh parsley, chopped
  Instructions:
1. Brown Meatballs: In a large pot, brown meatballs over medium heat, then remove and set aside.
2. Cook Vegetables: In the same pot, sauté onion and garlic until fragrant. Add carrots, potatoes, thyme, salt, and pepper.
3. Simmer: Add beef broth and return meatballs to the pot. Bring to a boil, reduce heat, and simmer for 20-25 minutes until potatoes are tender.
4. Serve: Garnish with chopped parsley and serve hot.

Korean BBQ Meatballs

Ingredients:

- 1 lb ground beef or pork
- 2 tbsp soy sauce
- 1 tbsp sesame oil
- 2 cloves garlic, minced
- 1 tsp ginger, grated
- 1 tbsp brown sugar
- 1 tbsp rice vinegar
- 2 tbsp green onions, chopped
- 1 tbsp sesame seeds

Instructions:

1. Mix Meatball Ingredients: In a bowl, combine ground meat, soy sauce, sesame oil, garlic, ginger, brown sugar, rice vinegar, and a pinch of salt. Shape into meatballs.
2. Cook Meatballs: Heat a skillet over medium-high heat and cook meatballs until browned on all sides and cooked through, about 8-10 minutes.
3. Serve: Garnish with chopped green onions and sesame seeds. Serve with rice or in lettuce wraps.

Parmesan and Ricotta Meatballs

Ingredients:

- 1 lb ground beef
- 1/2 cup ricotta cheese
- 1/4 cup grated Parmesan cheese
- 1/4 cup breadcrumbs
- 1 egg
- 1 tsp garlic powder
- 1 tsp dried basil
- Salt and pepper to taste

Instructions:

1. Mix Meatball Ingredients: In a bowl, combine ground beef, ricotta, Parmesan, breadcrumbs, egg, garlic powder, basil, salt, and pepper. Shape into meatballs.
2. Cook Meatballs: Bake meatballs in a preheated 375°F (190°C) oven for 15-20 minutes until golden and cooked through.
3. Serve: Serve with marinara sauce and a side of garlic bread or pasta.

Beef and Bacon Meatballs

Ingredients:

- 1 lb ground beef
- 1/2 lb bacon, chopped
- 1/4 cup breadcrumbs
- 1 egg
- 1 tsp garlic powder
- Salt and pepper to taste
- 1 tbsp olive oil

Instructions:

1. Cook Bacon: In a skillet, cook chopped bacon until crispy. Remove and set aside.
2. Mix Meatball Ingredients: In a bowl, combine ground beef, cooked bacon, breadcrumbs, egg, garlic powder, salt, and pepper. Shape into meatballs.
3. Cook Meatballs: Heat olive oil in a skillet over medium heat. Brown meatballs on all sides and cook through, about 8-10 minutes.
4. Serve: Serve with a side of roasted vegetables or on a bun for a meatball sandwich.

Sweet and Spicy Teriyaki Meatballs

Ingredients:

- 1 lb ground beef or chicken
- 1/4 cup breadcrumbs
- 1 egg
- 2 tbsp soy sauce
- 2 tbsp honey
- 2 tbsp rice vinegar
- 1 tbsp sriracha sauce
- 2 cloves garlic, minced
- 1 tsp ginger, grated
- 1 tbsp sesame oil
- 1 tbsp sesame seeds (for garnish)
- Green onions, chopped (for garnish)

Instructions:

1. **Prepare Meatballs**: In a bowl, combine ground meat, breadcrumbs, egg, garlic, and ginger. Shape into meatballs.
2. **Cook Meatballs**: Bake meatballs in a preheated 375°F (190°C) oven for 15-20 minutes until golden and cooked through.
3. **Make Sauce**: In a small saucepan, combine soy sauce, honey, rice vinegar, and sriracha. Bring to a simmer and cook for 3-5 minutes, until slightly thickened.
4. **Coat Meatballs**: Toss cooked meatballs in the teriyaki sauce.
5. **Serve**: Garnish with sesame seeds and green onions. Serve with rice or vegetables.

Lamb Meatballs with Feta and Olives

Ingredients:

- 1 lb ground lamb
- 1/4 cup feta cheese, crumbled
- 1/4 cup Kalamata olives, chopped
- 1/4 cup breadcrumbs
- 1 egg
- 1 tsp garlic powder
- 1 tsp dried oregano
- Salt and pepper to taste

Instructions:

1. **Mix Meatball Ingredients**: In a bowl, combine ground lamb, feta, olives, breadcrumbs, egg, garlic powder, oregano, salt, and pepper. Shape into meatballs.
2. **Cook Meatballs**: Heat olive oil in a skillet over medium heat and cook meatballs until browned on all sides and cooked through, about 8-10 minutes.
3. **Serve**: Serve with tzatziki sauce and a side of roasted vegetables or pita.

Italian Sausage and Beef Meatballs

Ingredients:

- 1/2 lb ground beef
- 1/2 lb Italian sausage (mild or spicy)
- 1/4 cup breadcrumbs
- 1/4 cup grated Parmesan cheese
- 1/2 tsp dried basil
- 1/2 tsp dried oregano
- 1 egg
- 1/2 cup marinara sauce

Instructions:

1. **Mix Meatball Ingredients**: In a bowl, combine ground beef, Italian sausage, breadcrumbs, Parmesan, basil, oregano, egg, salt, and pepper. Shape into meatballs.
2. **Cook Meatballs**: Heat olive oil in a skillet and cook meatballs over medium heat until browned on all sides and cooked through, about 10-12 minutes.
3. **Simmer in Sauce**: Add marinara sauce to the skillet, cover, and simmer for 10 minutes.
4. **Serve**: Serve with pasta or on sub rolls for meatball sandwiches.

Thai Chicken Meatballs with Peanut Sauce

Ingredients:

- 1 lb ground chicken
- 1/4 cup breadcrumbs
- 1 egg
- 2 tbsp soy sauce
- 1 tbsp fish sauce
- 1 tbsp fresh lime juice
- 1 tbsp cilantro, chopped
- 2 cloves garlic, minced
- 1 tbsp ginger, grated
- 1/4 cup peanut butter
- 1 tbsp soy sauce (for sauce)
- 1 tbsp honey (for sauce)
- 1 tbsp lime juice (for sauce)
- 1 tbsp water (for sauce)

Instructions:

1. **Prepare Meatballs**: In a bowl, combine ground chicken, breadcrumbs, egg, soy sauce, fish sauce, lime juice, cilantro, garlic, and ginger. Shape into meatballs.
2. **Cook Meatballs**: Bake meatballs in a preheated 375°F (190°C) oven for 15-20 minutes until golden and cooked through.
3. **Make Peanut Sauce**: In a bowl, whisk together peanut butter, soy sauce, honey, lime juice, and water until smooth.
4. **Serve**: Drizzle peanut sauce over meatballs and garnish with additional cilantro. Serve with rice or vegetables.

Meatball Soup with Veggies

Ingredients:

- 1 lb ground beef or turkey
- 1/4 cup breadcrumbs
- 1 egg
- 1/2 cup onion, chopped
- 2 carrots, diced
- 2 celery stalks, diced
- 4 cups beef or vegetable broth
- 1 can diced tomatoes
- 1 cup frozen peas
- 1 tsp dried thyme
- Salt and pepper to taste

Instructions:

1. **Make Meatballs**: In a bowl, combine ground meat, breadcrumbs, egg, salt, and pepper. Shape into small meatballs.
2. **Brown Meatballs**: In a large pot, brown meatballs over medium heat, then remove and set aside.
3. **Cook Veggies**: In the same pot, sauté onions, carrots, and celery until softened, about 5-7 minutes.
4. **Simmer Soup**: Add broth, diced tomatoes, peas, thyme, and meatballs to the pot. Bring to a boil, then simmer for 20 minutes until the meatballs are cooked through.
5. **Serve**: Serve hot with crusty bread.

Almond-Crusted Meatballs

Ingredients:

- 1 lb ground chicken or turkey
- 1/4 cup almond flour
- 1/4 cup grated Parmesan cheese
- 1 egg
- 1 tsp garlic powder
- 1 tsp dried rosemary
- Salt and pepper to taste
- 1/4 cup almond slices (for coating)

Instructions:

1. **Mix Meatball Ingredients**: In a bowl, combine ground meat, almond flour, Parmesan, egg, garlic powder, rosemary, salt, and pepper. Shape into meatballs.
2. **Coat Meatballs**: Roll meatballs in almond slices until well coated.
3. **Cook Meatballs**: Bake meatballs in a preheated 375°F (190°C) oven for 15-20 minutes until golden and cooked through.
4. **Serve**: Serve with a side of roasted vegetables or in a salad.

Asian-style Turkey Meatballs

Ingredients:

- 1 lb ground turkey
- 1/4 cup breadcrumbs
- 1 egg
- 2 tbsp soy sauce
- 1 tbsp sesame oil
- 1 tbsp fresh ginger, grated
- 2 cloves garlic, minced
- 2 tbsp green onions, chopped
- 1 tbsp sesame seeds (for garnish)

Instructions:

1. **Prepare Meatballs**: In a bowl, combine ground turkey, breadcrumbs, egg, soy sauce, sesame oil, ginger, garlic, and green onions. Shape into meatballs.
2. **Cook Meatballs**: Bake meatballs in a preheated 375°F (190°C) oven for 15-20 minutes until cooked through.
3. **Serve**: Garnish with sesame seeds and serve with rice or in lettuce wraps.

Italian Meatballs with Peppers and Onions

Ingredients:

- 1 lb ground beef
- 1/4 cup breadcrumbs
- 1/4 cup grated Parmesan cheese
- 1/2 tsp dried oregano
- 1 egg
- 2 bell peppers, sliced
- 1 onion, sliced
- 2 cups marinara sauce

Instructions:

1. **Prepare Meatballs**: In a bowl, combine ground beef, breadcrumbs, Parmesan, oregano, egg, salt, and pepper. Shape into meatballs.
2. **Cook Meatballs**: In a large skillet, brown meatballs over medium heat, then remove and set aside.
3. **Cook Veggies**: In the same skillet, sauté peppers and onions until softened.
4. **Simmer**: Add marinara sauce and meatballs back into the skillet. Simmer for 10-15 minutes until meatballs are cooked through.
5. **Serve**: Serve meatballs and vegetables with pasta or on a sub roll.

Spicy Chorizo Meatballs

Ingredients:

- 1 lb chorizo sausage, casings removed
- 1/4 cup breadcrumbs
- 1 egg
- 1/2 tsp chili flakes
- 1 tsp cumin
- 1/2 tsp paprika
- 2 cloves garlic, minced
- Salt and pepper to taste

Instructions:

1. **Mix Meatball Ingredients**: In a bowl, combine chorizo, breadcrumbs, egg, chili flakes, cumin, paprika, garlic, salt, and pepper. Shape into meatballs.
2. **Cook Meatballs**: Heat olive oil in a skillet and cook meatballs over medium heat until browned on all sides and cooked through, about 8-10 minutes.
3. **Serve**: Serve with a side of rice or in a tortilla for a spicy taco.

Swedish Meatballs with Lingonberry Sauce

Ingredients:

- 1 lb ground beef
- 1/2 lb ground pork
- 1/4 cup breadcrumbs
- 1/4 cup milk
- 1 egg
- 1 small onion, finely chopped
- 1 tsp salt
- 1/2 tsp black pepper
- 1/4 tsp allspice
- 1/4 tsp nutmeg
- 2 tbsp butter (for cooking)
- 1/2 cup beef broth
- 1/4 cup heavy cream
- 1/4 cup lingonberry jam

Instructions:

1. **Make Meatballs**: In a bowl, combine ground beef, ground pork, breadcrumbs, milk, egg, onion, salt, pepper, allspice, and nutmeg. Shape into small meatballs.
2. **Cook Meatballs**: Heat butter in a skillet over medium heat and cook meatballs until browned on all sides and cooked through, about 8-10 minutes.
3. **Make Sauce**: Remove meatballs from skillet, then add beef broth and heavy cream to the skillet. Simmer for a few minutes until thickened.
4. **Serve**: Add meatballs back to the skillet and coat with the sauce. Serve with lingonberry jam on the side.

Beef and Pork Meatballs with Garlic Butter

Ingredients:

- 1 lb ground beef
- 1/2 lb ground pork
- 1/4 cup breadcrumbs
- 1 egg
- 1/2 cup grated Parmesan cheese
- 1 tsp garlic powder
- Salt and pepper to taste
- 4 tbsp butter
- 4 cloves garlic, minced
- 1 tbsp fresh parsley, chopped

Instructions:

1. **Make Meatballs**: In a bowl, combine ground beef, ground pork, breadcrumbs, egg, Parmesan, garlic powder, salt, and pepper. Shape into meatballs.
2. **Cook Meatballs**: Heat olive oil in a skillet over medium heat and cook meatballs until browned on all sides and cooked through, about 10 minutes.
3. **Make Garlic Butter**: In the same skillet, melt butter and sauté garlic for 1-2 minutes until fragrant.
4. **Serve**: Coat meatballs with the garlic butter sauce and sprinkle with fresh parsley.

BBQ Chicken Meatballs

Ingredients:

- 1 lb ground chicken
- 1/4 cup breadcrumbs
- 1 egg
- 1/2 cup shredded cheddar cheese
- 1/4 cup BBQ sauce (plus extra for coating)
- 1 tsp smoked paprika
- Salt and pepper to taste

Instructions:

1. **Make Meatballs**: In a bowl, combine ground chicken, breadcrumbs, egg, cheddar cheese, BBQ sauce, paprika, salt, and pepper. Shape into meatballs.
2. **Cook Meatballs**: Bake meatballs in a preheated 375°F (190°C) oven for 15-20 minutes until golden and cooked through.
3. **Coat with BBQ Sauce**: Brush cooked meatballs with additional BBQ sauce and bake for an additional 5 minutes.
4. **Serve**: Serve with extra BBQ sauce for dipping or over a bed of coleslaw.

Spaghetti and Meatballs

Ingredients:

- 1 lb ground beef
- 1/2 lb ground pork
- 1/4 cup breadcrumbs
- 1/4 cup grated Parmesan cheese
- 1/4 cup fresh parsley, chopped
- 1 egg
- 2 cups marinara sauce
- 1 lb spaghetti
- Salt and pepper to taste

Instructions:

1. **Make Meatballs**: In a bowl, combine ground beef, ground pork, breadcrumbs, Parmesan, parsley, egg, salt, and pepper. Shape into meatballs.
2. **Cook Meatballs**: Heat olive oil in a skillet over medium heat and cook meatballs until browned on all sides and cooked through, about 10-12 minutes.
3. **Simmer in Sauce**: Add marinara sauce to the skillet and simmer for 10-15 minutes.
4. **Cook Spaghetti**: Cook spaghetti according to package instructions.
5. **Serve**: Serve meatballs and sauce over cooked spaghetti with extra Parmesan on top.

Zesty Cilantro Lime Meatballs

Ingredients:

- 1 lb ground turkey
- 1/4 cup breadcrumbs
- 1 egg
- 1/2 cup fresh cilantro, chopped
- Zest and juice of 1 lime
- 1/2 tsp cumin
- Salt and pepper to taste
- 2 tbsp olive oil (for cooking)

Instructions:

1. **Make Meatballs**: In a bowl, combine ground turkey, breadcrumbs, egg, cilantro, lime zest, lime juice, cumin, salt, and pepper. Shape into meatballs.
2. **Cook Meatballs**: Heat olive oil in a skillet over medium heat and cook meatballs until browned on all sides and cooked through, about 8-10 minutes.
3. **Serve**: Serve with a side of rice or in lettuce wraps with extra lime wedges.

Coconut Curry Meatballs

Ingredients:

- 1 lb ground chicken
- 1/4 cup breadcrumbs
- 1 egg
- 2 tbsp curry powder
- 1/2 cup coconut milk
- 1/4 cup cilantro, chopped
- 1/2 tsp salt
- 1/4 tsp black pepper
- 2 tbsp olive oil (for cooking)

Instructions:

1. **Make Meatballs**: In a bowl, combine ground chicken, breadcrumbs, egg, curry powder, coconut milk, cilantro, salt, and pepper. Shape into meatballs.
2. **Cook Meatballs**: Heat olive oil in a skillet over medium heat and cook meatballs until browned on all sides and cooked through, about 10 minutes.
3. **Serve**: Serve with rice and a drizzle of additional coconut milk or curry sauce.

Cajun Shrimp Meatballs

Ingredients:

- 1 lb shrimp, peeled and deveined
- 1/4 cup breadcrumbs
- 1 egg
- 1 tbsp Cajun seasoning
- 2 cloves garlic, minced
- 1/4 cup green onions, chopped
- 2 tbsp olive oil (for cooking)

Instructions:

1. **Prepare Shrimp**: Pulse shrimp in a food processor until finely chopped.
2. **Make Meatballs**: In a bowl, combine chopped shrimp, breadcrumbs, egg, Cajun seasoning, garlic, green onions, salt, and pepper. Shape into meatballs.
3. **Cook Meatballs**: Heat olive oil in a skillet over medium heat and cook meatballs until browned on all sides and cooked through, about 5-7 minutes.
4. **Serve**: Serve with a side of spicy dipping sauce or over a bed of rice.

Meatball and Polenta Bake

Ingredients:

- 1 lb ground beef
- 1/2 lb ground pork
- 1/4 cup breadcrumbs
- 1 egg
- 1/2 cup grated Parmesan cheese
- 2 cups marinara sauce
- 2 cups cooked polenta
- 1/2 cup shredded mozzarella cheese
- Salt and pepper to taste

Instructions:

1. **Make Meatballs**: In a bowl, combine ground beef, ground pork, breadcrumbs, egg, Parmesan, salt, and pepper. Shape into meatballs.
2. **Cook Meatballs**: Heat olive oil in a skillet over medium heat and cook meatballs until browned on all sides and cooked through, about 8-10 minutes.
3. **Assemble the Bake**: Preheat the oven to 375°F (190°C). In a baking dish, layer the cooked polenta, top with marinara sauce, and then arrange the meatballs on top.
4. **Top with Cheese**: Sprinkle shredded mozzarella over the top and bake for 15-20 minutes, until the cheese is melted and bubbly.
5. **Serve**: Serve hot, garnished with fresh basil or parsley.

Classic Beef Meatballs in Gravy

Ingredients:

- 1 lb ground beef
- 1/4 cup breadcrumbs
- 1 egg
- 1 small onion, finely chopped
- 2 cloves garlic, minced
- 1/2 tsp salt
- 1/4 tsp black pepper
- 1 tbsp olive oil (for frying)
- 2 cups beef broth
- 2 tbsp flour
- 1/4 cup heavy cream

Instructions:

1. **Make Meatballs**: In a bowl, combine ground beef, breadcrumbs, egg, onion, garlic, salt, and pepper. Shape into meatballs.
2. **Cook Meatballs**: Heat olive oil in a skillet over medium heat and cook meatballs until browned on all sides and cooked through, about 8-10 minutes.
3. **Make Gravy**: In the same skillet, remove the meatballs and add flour to the drippings, stirring to make a roux. Slowly whisk in beef broth, then simmer until thickened. Stir in heavy cream and adjust seasoning.
4. **Serve**: Return meatballs to the skillet and coat with gravy. Serve with mashed potatoes or rice.

Moroccan-Spiced Beef Meatballs

Ingredients:

- 1 lb ground beef
- 1/4 cup breadcrumbs
- 1 egg
- 1 tsp ground cumin
- 1 tsp ground cinnamon
- 1/2 tsp ground coriander
- 2 cloves garlic, minced
- 2 tbsp fresh parsley, chopped
- 1/4 cup raisins
- Salt and pepper to taste
- 2 tbsp olive oil (for cooking)

Instructions:

1. **Make Meatballs**: In a bowl, combine ground beef, breadcrumbs, egg, cumin, cinnamon, coriander, garlic, parsley, raisins, salt, and pepper. Shape into meatballs.
2. **Cook Meatballs**: Heat olive oil in a skillet over medium heat and cook meatballs until browned on all sides and cooked through, about 8-10 minutes.
3. **Serve**: Serve with couscous, roasted vegetables, or a yogurt dipping sauce.

Italian Meatballs in a Red Wine Sauce

Ingredients:

- 1 lb ground beef
- 1/2 lb ground pork
- 1/4 cup breadcrumbs
- 1 egg
- 1/2 cup grated Parmesan cheese
- 1 tsp dried oregano
- 1 tsp garlic powder
- 2 cups marinara sauce
- 1/2 cup red wine
- Fresh basil for garnish
  Instructions:
1. **Make Meatballs**: In a bowl, combine ground beef, ground pork, breadcrumbs, egg, Parmesan, oregano, garlic powder, salt, and pepper. Shape into meatballs.
2. **Cook Meatballs**: Heat olive oil in a skillet over medium heat and cook meatballs until browned on all sides and cooked through, about 8-10 minutes.
3. **Make Sauce**: In the same skillet, add marinara sauce and red wine, stirring to combine. Simmer for 10 minutes, allowing the sauce to thicken.
4. **Serve**: Return meatballs to the sauce and simmer for an additional 10 minutes. Garnish with fresh basil and serve with pasta or crusty bread.

Sweet Chili Chicken Meatballs

Ingredients:

- 1 lb ground chicken
- 1/4 cup breadcrumbs
- 1 egg
- 2 tbsp sweet chili sauce
- 1 tbsp soy sauce
- 1/2 tsp garlic powder
- 1/4 tsp ground ginger
- 1 tbsp sesame oil (for cooking)
- 2 tbsp fresh cilantro, chopped

Instructions:

1. **Make Meatballs**: In a bowl, combine ground chicken, breadcrumbs, egg, sweet chili sauce, soy sauce, garlic powder, ginger, and salt. Shape into meatballs.
2. **Cook Meatballs**: Heat sesame oil in a skillet over medium heat and cook meatballs until browned on all sides and cooked through, about 8-10 minutes.
3. **Serve**: Garnish with fresh cilantro and serve with steamed rice or stir-fried vegetables.

Pork and Apple Meatballs

Ingredients:

- 1 lb ground pork
- 1/2 apple, grated
- 1/4 cup breadcrumbs
- 1 egg
- 1 tsp ground cinnamon
- 1/4 tsp ground nutmeg
- 2 cloves garlic, minced
- Salt and pepper to taste
- 2 tbsp olive oil (for frying)

Instructions:

1. **Make Meatballs**: In a bowl, combine ground pork, grated apple, breadcrumbs, egg, cinnamon, nutmeg, garlic, salt, and pepper. Shape into meatballs.
2. **Cook Meatballs**: Heat olive oil in a skillet over medium heat and cook meatballs until browned on all sides and cooked through, about 8-10 minutes.
3. **Serve**: Serve with a side of mashed potatoes or a fresh salad.

Cilantro and Lime Pork Meatballs

Ingredients:

- 1 lb ground pork
- 1/4 cup fresh cilantro, chopped
- Zest and juice of 1 lime
- 1/4 cup breadcrumbs
- 1 egg
- 2 cloves garlic, minced
- Salt and pepper to taste
- 2 tbsp olive oil (for frying)

Instructions:

1. **Make Meatballs**: In a bowl, combine ground pork, cilantro, lime zest, lime juice, breadcrumbs, egg, garlic, salt, and pepper. Shape into meatballs.
2. **Cook Meatballs**: Heat olive oil in a skillet over medium heat and cook meatballs until browned on all sides and cooked through, about 8-10 minutes.
3. **Serve**: Serve with a lime wedge and a side of Mexican rice or a light salad.

Meatball Bolognese

Ingredients:

- 1 lb ground beef
- 1/2 lb ground pork
- 1/4 cup breadcrumbs
- 1 egg
- 2 tbsp fresh parsley, chopped
- 2 cloves garlic, minced
- 1 onion, finely chopped
- 2 cups marinara sauce
- 1/2 cup red wine
- Salt and pepper to taste

Instructions:

1. **Make Meatballs**: In a bowl, combine ground beef, ground pork, breadcrumbs, egg, parsley, garlic, salt, and pepper. Shape into meatballs.
2. **Cook Meatballs**: Heat olive oil in a skillet over medium heat and cook meatballs until browned on all sides and cooked through, about 8-10 minutes.
3. **Make Bolognese Sauce**: In the same skillet, sauté onion and garlic until softened. Add red wine and let it reduce by half. Add marinara sauce and bring to a simmer.
4. **Serve**: Return meatballs to the sauce and simmer for 15-20 minutes. Serve over pasta or with crusty bread.

Mediterranean Lamb Meatballs

Ingredients:

- 1 lb ground lamb
- 1/4 cup breadcrumbs
- 1 egg
- 2 tbsp fresh parsley, chopped
- 1 tsp ground cumin
- 1 tsp ground coriander
- 1/2 tsp ground cinnamon
- 2 cloves garlic, minced
- Salt and pepper to taste
- 2 tbsp olive oil (for frying)
- 1/2 cup tzatziki sauce

Instructions:

1. **Make Meatballs**: In a bowl, combine ground lamb, breadcrumbs, egg, parsley, cumin, coriander, cinnamon, garlic, salt, and pepper. Shape into meatballs.
2. **Cook Meatballs**: Heat olive oil in a skillet over medium heat and cook meatballs until browned on all sides and cooked through, about 8-10 minutes.
3. **Serve**: Serve with a side of tzatziki sauce and a Greek salad or pita bread.

Grilled Beef Meatballs with Chimichurri

Ingredients:

- 1 lb ground beef
- 1/4 cup breadcrumbs
- 1 egg
- 1 tbsp fresh parsley, chopped
- 1 tsp dried oregano
- 2 cloves garlic, minced
- Salt and pepper to taste
- 2 tbsp olive oil (for grilling)
- **For Chimichurri**:
    - 1/2 cup fresh parsley
    - 2 tbsp red wine vinegar
    - 1/4 cup olive oil
    - 1 tsp red pepper flakes
    - 2 cloves garlic, minced
    - Salt and pepper to taste

Instructions:

1. **Make Meatballs**: In a bowl, combine ground beef, breadcrumbs, egg, parsley, oregano, garlic, salt, and pepper. Shape into meatballs.
2. **Grill Meatballs**: Preheat the grill to medium heat. Brush the meatballs with olive oil and grill for 6-8 minutes, turning occasionally, until cooked through.
3. **Make Chimichurri**: In a bowl, combine parsley, red wine vinegar, olive oil, red pepper flakes, garlic, salt, and pepper. Mix well.
4. **Serve**: Drizzle chimichurri sauce over the grilled meatballs and serve with grilled vegetables or a fresh salad.

www.ingramcontent.com/pod-product-compliance
Lightning Source LLC
LaVergne TN
LVHW081507060526
838201LV00056BA/2986